I AM A BROKEN HOUSE

I AM A BROKEN HOUSE

A Collection of Poetry

J. PATRICK LEMARR

write crowd
publishing

WRITE CROWD PUBLISHING

www.writecrowdpublishing.com

Credits

Cover Design and Write Crowd Publishing logo courtesy of Chip Smitson.

Illustration "Enter In" courtesy of Jason Webb.
www.webb-headz.com

Author photos courtesy of Holly Thrasher.
www.capturedbythrasher.com

The author wishes to thank: Jan Loy, Shelly Dewitt, and Dr. Paul Lynch for title suggestions, Heidi Lemarr for editing assistance, and Tom and Patty Lemarr for their encouragement and support.

TIZA, karabin9 and **Orial** fonts used with permission.

terrible. 2011. In *Merriam-Webster.com*.
Retrieved June 16, 2011, from http://www.merriam-webster.com/dictionary/terrible

FIRST EDITION

ISBN 978-0-9838337-2-7

17 16 15 14 13 12 ° 2 3 4 5 6 7

For my wife, as lovely as she is wise.

For my daughters, my angels of mercy.

For my son, a most welcome addition.

"It is strange how often a heart must be broken before the years can make it wise." — Sara Teasdale

"Suffering has been stronger than all other teaching, and has taught me to understand what your heart used to be. I have been bent and broken, but - I hope - into a better shape." — Charles Dickens

CONTENTS

FOREWORD

This book earned its title in every conceivable way. When I first began planning its publication, I had no way of knowing it would turn out to be such an uphill climb during one of the most hellishly trying seasons of my life. It seemed, after all, like an easy enough task: collect the poetry I had written over the course of the last few years, present it to the world and hope that it would eventually recoup its cost. That's really all I envisioned for it. Easy peasy.

John Lennon wrote "life is what happens to you while you're busy making other plans," and as I assembled my team—the incredible Chip Smitson to design my book cover, artist Jason Webb to craft a simple, elegant interior image, and photographer Holly Thrasher, who had the unenviable task of trying to make me look good on the back cover—life just rattled past me like a train of thought with no engineer at its controls. In hindsight that was no truer then than it is ever true. The Great Engineer was and remains always at the helm. But several years later, I stagger at the realization of just how many obstacles nearly kept this book simmering away into nothingness on the back burner of my life.

The details of my struggles are not worth delving into at this point, although some of them certainly worked their way into the poetry you are about to read. To share details now would only anchor you deep within *my* journey…and what interests me is *our* journey.

We all have been broken. We all have suffered loss. We all have endured the dire seasons of this life and will, with the grace of God, endure many more. Such seasons and the ways we go about surviving them help refine and define us, whether for better or worse. In that refining fire, we learn how strong a foundation our friendships have been built upon, that our true family is often born of something deeper than blood, and that our faith, if indeed we've been graced with some, grows stronger in the midst of our weakness. For that reason, brokenness is as much a cause for celebration as any victory.

I am broken. This book is broken. You, dear friend, are broken. And it is in our brokenness that we become something new…something better.

May we be broken in all the right places.

J. Patrick Lemarr
October 2011

CONNOISSEUR: AN INVOCATION

Sip me
like a Sauvignon.
Take your precious time.
Swish me 'round
your luscious tongue,
my sommelier sublime.

Pour me
for the commonwealth.
Issue my reserve.
Make a toast
to verbal health,
that vintage seldom served.

THE LIAR

her mouth's a trap for foolish rats
her tongue, its rancid cheese
her god, a phallic idol that she worships on her knees
her words are built of cyanide
her thoughts, disease and smoke
each unintended sliver of truth,
       the grit on which she chokes

her eyes are broken monitors
that see in bits and bytes
her soul, a withered husk of kerosene and dynamite
her jumbled teeth are match heads
and tombstones for her kiss
she wears spite like a cloisonné pin
       and speaks with bark and hiss

UNSPOKEN TRUTH

it hung in the air between us
the truth behind the pain
unuttered, unattempted
mauled by grief untamed

we drifted like the continents
Pangea but a dream
destructing, deconstructing
oceans left between

ACHE BEAUTIFUL

Night gave way
to hope's true warmth—
a pleasant burn I pray will never heal.
I long to remain blistered,
wounded as I am by grace,
altered as I am by mercy's dirge.

My mind cannot comprehend
or grasp
or clutch
the pure elixir of meaning,
the knowledge of heaven,
of earth and hell,
and hell on earth.

I've searched under couch cushions,
beneath holy socks
and thread-worn underwear
in the drawer
in the bureau
in the closet
in the room
in the house
where I live and move and have my being,
searching for the change…
the ransom required to step forward
into the source of hope's warmth—
the ONE
whose mercy is made new
each day.

RESURRECTION

I fell to earth—
a rumor,
a wisp of things unsaid, unseen, unsettling—
with hope that
ONE
might speak my name
and bring the dead to life.

I walk the Earth—
a specter,
a ghost of things buried below believing—
with faith that
one
might speak His name
and bring the dead to life.

BURY ME IN
FAMILIAR THINGS

bury me in familiar things
in the clothes I wear and a wedding ring
shroud me in what came before
in a quiet sigh and a beastly roar

mark me with the pocks of time
three meters deep in bastard rhyme
lay lilies on my nighttime haunt
where I'm consumed by need and want

bury me in the earth I loathe
in my Friday lies and my Sunday clothes

I AM A BROKEN HOUSE

I am a perfectly broken house
condemned to stand empty—
my nakedness covered only by the grim caress
of sumac and scrub,
fireman ladders for the ants and huntsman spiders
who do their business in my bones.

I speak in stuttered clacks.
Shutters crack against my shattered eyes—
sightless now to all but rot.
Grackles cluster in my dusty mind,
bickering back and forth
about the arid sky.

My joints protest every insolent draft.
Rusty tears stain their memories upon my walls.
Stories live there still—
echoes on the deafened ears
of ghosts
that seldom come to call.

ISOLATION

bloody numb, those bastard thoughts
that someone else's mind has wrought
and dumb the mouth of dead cliché
that speaks of stars by light of day

so deaf the ears that cannot hear
the fleeting truth you seek and fear
and dead the heart that cannot bear
the love your sleeve would gladly wear

HER SATIN LIPS
ON WHICH I REST

her satin lips on which I rest
my gentle sigh at her behest
betray the pounding in her chest
and bring to mind this one request

that if I should not know her flesh
the lingered joy of her caress
perhaps it would be for the best
for God not to have carved the breast

for every slope and curve is still
the rise and fall of every thrill
and though my lust true faith should kill
I cannot bear that bitter pill

for loathe am I to scorn the skin
each naked glimpse that reels me in
and if desire be truly sin
it is the pot I'm stewing in

MY MISTRESS DARK

Insomnia, my mistress dark,
who stains my windows, poisons art—
madness you have sown within
this waking dream I'm living in.

Insomnia, my lover cruel,
who prostitutes to wise and fool—
madness you transfuse again
in palsied hand, in ink of pen.

Insomnia, my loathsome bride,
who dams my thoughts, my hopeless tide—
madness you reveal as sin
yet, madder still, I pay again.

DISCONNECT

if my mind can ever grasp
what my heart already knows
I might not spend each evening
in the company of ghosts
playing out the might-have-beens,
cruel what-ifs and such
unspoken things we meant to say
and each neglected touch

if my mind can only brush
but the hem of my Heart's robe
I'll see myself as shepherd king
and less as poor ol' Job
living in the wreckage of
a grace that once was mine
instead of facing giants
sure of victory divine

if my mind ever arrives
where my heart already dwells
I'll rest in unearned heavens
instead of bartered hells
sleeping with the ichthus
in light that shall not dim
and not within a bowl of wrath
I filled just past its brim

OL' ANDREW

ol' Andrew, he sawr Elliphants
whene'er he drunk his wine
for two bottles, four bottles, sometimes six
would drink he at a time

a fist he'd throw at friend or bro
as though they'd boned his maw
when all they ever done him wrong
was calling down the law

ol' Andrew'd spend the night in jail
they'd let him out come nine
then two bottles, four bottles, sometimes six
would drink he of his wine

SURREALITY

slowly she slips
beneath a sea of satin
        a sinful shark
          circling another savage
     soul; a silent
succubus, serene
and
seductive
       soundlessly snaking
       through slipshod
   resolve;
a sexual
spirit—my sword
     her stolen
         souvenir

VACUUM

rabbi with no temple
bishop without Rome
I have come undone—
a life in monochrome

shadows have more substance
whispers more to shout
napalm less destruction
atheists less doubt

guru with no mantra
healer with no hands
I am deathly worn—
a cord of broken strands

inkblots hold more meaning
paupers more to share
Peter less denial
Atlas less to bear

preacher with no pulpit
prophet without dreams
I am just a hole—
a vacuum in old jeans

I WAS PRAYING FOR RAIN
WHEN THE FLOOD
CAME

I was praying for rain when the flood came
wishing for a drop when the sky caved in
I was dying of thirst when the flood came
—a deluge of Your terrible grace

I was dreaming of a breeze when the storm came
Katrina and the waves bent on waging war
I was longing for the wind when the storm came
—inception of near limitless change

I was praying for peace when the grief came
desperate for Your strength when my world crashed
        down
I was praising Your name when the grief came
—a deluge of Your terrible grace

---

ter·ri·ble

1 a : exciting extreme alarm or intense fear :
TERRIFYING
  b : formidable in nature : AWESOME
  c : DIFFICULT

COLD CHINESE

She boxes me up
like cold Chinese
with words
and stares
in Frigidaires
of mothballed expectation.

She molds the package
to fit her lies
of faith
and sin
to do me in
with twilight revelation.

ANTICIPATION

she ripens in the darkness
fruit of night
anxious for dew

desperate for teeth
to pierce purple flesh
and lips to drink of nectar
growing sweeter by the hour

he withers in the sunlight
clothed in mud
anxious for shade

hungry for the waste
(decadent decay)
or, better still, some nectar
'fore the fallen fruit grows sour

LIQUIDGRACE

liquidgrace exits the wound
homeless man dying from womb
finite and infinite
fleshbone messiah
33yearold
temple pariah
weaponless peacenik
merciful savior
God/man of sorrows
gentle doubtslayer

SHE'S THE LEVEL MIRROR

she's the level mirror
of the fountain I am fishing
receiving tender minnows
and the chaos coins of wishing

she's the marble bathhouse
for those filthy birds of prey
who shield themselves from iron eaves
reflecting light of day

every sixpence that I drown
sends ripples through her surface
as though the paltry weight of it
could ever viands purchase

yet she is where I linger
in this garden of remember
forever filling pockets
with the coins which now offend her

BEAUTIFUL STRANGER

I pissed away what passed for grace
(a darkened glass, a holy face)
and fell for knockoffs built of rust,
fictitious gods of fumes and dust.

I cried dead tears that laid to waste
the love I'd overlooked in haste—
that gentle touch of Someone more
I'd left unanswered at the door.

VANITY IS THE DRUG
OF CHOICE

a Cheshire grin is plastered on her pretty, plastic face
her spray-on gown as sexy as her sighs
her hollow thoughts are hidden by her high-end haute
    couture
a predator who preens for public eyes

a siren song is slipping through her collagen and MAC
a pretty lie that lingers on her lips
she pacifies the party with her paparazzi sneer
she hypnotizes husbands with her hips

her champagne charms are cherished by the chandelier
    elite
a vicious Venus, vain and self-adored
her folly ever focused on the fashionista teat
her heart is but a hanger for her lord

PRITHEE, WARM THINE ABSINTHE THOUGHTS

prithee, warm thine absinthe thoughts
o'er my wicked flame
let fables spill and ease the chill
of heaven's cruel game

poets sow their maudlin dreams
in papyrus fields
thus reaping there each stanza fair
their blessed hubris yields

prithee, wash thine absinthe thoughts
down with water sweet
let meter force the artist's course
to heaven's own heartbeat

TENTATIVE

Tentative—
these fingers mine
that sweep the landscape of your spine,
between your shoulders as you lie,
and in the valley of your sigh.

Tentative—
these fingertips
that drink you in with treasured sips
and marvel at the grand design
that moved you from your bed to mine.

Tentative—
these fingers trace
the sleeping form of matchless grace.

Tentative—
with nightly fear
I'll break the spell that holds you here.

DAWN COMES
TO THE SLEEPLESS

somewhere in the waking world
a seraph haunts my dreams
surfing on the airwaves
and satellitic beams

perching on my brainstem
like Edgar's demon bird
nevermore to flutter
much less utter gracious word

saintly apparitions cast
their blind eyes to my fate
the faithful and the fallen
and his wordplay second-rate

the cherub pisses indigo
on worlds I would give breath
a sea of stench and stutter
that the penman knows is death

out there in a rested mind
an angel haunts each thought
pouncing on allusions
that, come dusk, shall all be rot

TO THE FLOCK AT ST. STARBUCKS EVANGELICAL CHURCH OF CONSERVATIVE TRUTH

how sweet the smell of your success
how warm the pride within your breast
and dead the Word upon your tongue
and all its living hope made dung

how dear the praise of God's right wing
how sure the grace of which you sing
though it's a truth you've never earned
and on your altar captives burned

bound to sin they cannot lose
I wonder, then, of your excuse
whose desert soul once tasted grace
and mercy's rain upon your face

how cold the fire left to your care
how cruel the law by which you swear
and dark the light He meant to shine
still trapped in mazes you design

how dead the life that you pretend
how tepid hearts of whitewashed men
who built a brand and sold it cheap
forsook the Shepherd for the sheep

THE QUIET ROOM

my mother died on a Thursday
      a Thursday, just a Thursday
not a holiday or a holy day
      just a Thursday
when she died

56, for 10
days, just 56 and one
mighty strong woman at that
8 days past my birthday
she died on a Thursday
when I least expected

she'd had a stroke, a terrible stroke
two days before my wedding
a terrible stroke
then wheelchairs and walkers
blood work and doctors
a slur in her speech
from a terrible stroke

5 months then
of struggle and strain
a family renewed by her struggle
and strain
5 months
of thinking things would be
okay

she held my hand
      on Thursday, when I least expected

emergency surgery and recovery time
but she recovered fine
      until that Thursday
when she said she was scared
I told her she would be fine
      I believed it
            I did
I really did

but so fast, too fast for my mind to catch up
there were doctors
and nurses
and fear and
      a chaplain and
a quiet room
where I held her hand
      and said things, not enough
things, but the important ones
the words that matter
in the quiet room

she left me there
alone with my boiling tears
      one fell to her hand
as I kissed it
      in the quiet room
where she left me alone
to go find my father and hers
      and her mother, who I barely knew

she left me there
      in the quiet room

and part of me remains

INDELIBLE MARKER

every son is heaven's own
not vagrants drunk on mayhem
wastes of air and blood and bone
the monsters we have made them

we bind them here
with doubt and fear
our hate's the damning clue
an indelible marker paints
a grim and vile tattoo

every light is heaven's light
yet we live in denial
where grace is weakness, might is right
and mercy is on trial

with doubt and fear
we bind them here
and, Heaven, help us all
an indelible marker paints
the pride before our fall

OF THE FORMER

there is a poison in my soul
which found me with a kiss
a delusional control
overridden by this
for the culprit I accuse
is a woman of ice
who will ravage your soul
without thinking twice

it was she that first taught me
what it means to know pain
like the ocean knows moonglow
and the jungle knows rain
so I beg you…consider
when pledging heart with kiss
she may treasure for a moment
then break with a twist

THE BEAUTIFUL LADY
IN THE BLACKBERRY
HAT

told, she did, her paramour
that all things lovely, right and pure
are due philosophy *du jour*
fanaticism's lure

said, she did, its wicked grip
could all archaic myths make slip
then every shred of faith will strip
and bloody reason's lip

told, she did, her lover new
what good a deadened heart can do
to fools who steep in moral stew
on some forgotten pew

said, she did, that God is dead
slain by those of learned head
who opted for His flesh instead
of prayer and daily bread

IN THE RAFTERS

somewhere in the rafters
in the space
where stories live
and poems hang upside down
like fruit bats
is the boy I used to be
(thought I was,
pretended to be)
disco dead
hollow as a gourd

somewhere in the crawlspace
in the dust
of former lives
where angels are hungry moths
with fierce mouths
is the boy I used to be
(hoped I was,
intended to be)
marble cold
fragile as the truth

somewhere in the cobwebs
in the waste
of yesterday
the decay of meant-to-be's
and cruel fate
is the boy I used to be
(feared I was,
despaired I would be)
haunted still
constant as regret

SHE DRIFTS ME LAZY

she drifts me lazy…this fallen-leaf man
with a change in his pocket and a dream in his hand
she steers me crazy to my destined knees
where I pray that I can be the man she sees

I mumble softly my songs of fear
making fumbled sense in my beauty's ear
I linger softly on her perfume breeze
and pray that I can be the man she sees

she steals me slowly…this zirconium man
with a body of dust and a brain full of sand
she peels me wholly from this costume I wear
with her nighttime eyes and her raven hair

I falter often with this mind of flight
even as we soar past the Northern Lights
I shed my coffin for a love so rare
with her nighttime eyes and her raven hair

VINCENT

the shape, the line, the thinning brush
        the twitch of palsied hands
the sheaves of wheat and starry nights
        the threat of Paul Gauguin

the fear of failure, lonely nights
        their sum was loss of mind
each dash and stroke, a little weight
        off shoulders too confined

'til, in the end, the truth occurred
        an end to all your pain
could not be found on this dread earth
        where struggle all in vain

but somewhere out beyond the veil
        the heaven of your dreams
where every effort would prevail
        against your saddest themes

DAMAGED GOODS

damaged goods
driven
by phallic
~~compulsionneurosispassionmaniapreoccupation~~obsession
needles, cigarettes and straws
of coke—cock
when the allusions
became illusions

ravaged goods
given
to tragic
aggression
feeble epithets and flaws
of deed—dead
among the living
and unforgiving

LAST AND LEAST

last and least
the little beasts
who fight for our attention
cannot attain
their longed-for fame
and pass on without mention

first and best
the doubly blessed
those haughty lords and ladies
will first and best be
'fore the rest
to pace the floor of Hades

SHE'S A DESERT CRAWL

she's a desert crawl
I am the fade of her oasis
a shining knight who cannot see
the dirt of peasant faces
she likes to imagine
that my heart is not a cancer
as though, by asking questions,
she can prove there is an answer

she's a little lamb
I am the wolf that comes a'prowling
with a wicked sense of humor
and a throat of constant growling
she commits to memory
every line that I stop humming
as though the songs we're moving to
contain the same dead drumming

she's a honey blonde
I wear the halo of dissension
some cruel joke that breaks the yoke
of unwanted attention
she likes to ignore the way
I mock my own undoing
fixing fast the lovely things
that I keep on ungluing

RAVAGED NUN
AND GREASY PRIEST

I tense like a tabby cat whose prey just flitted by
on paper wings
as thin as hope's blue thread

her grin—a feint
her teeth—capped with ice
topsy-turvy tombstones
of truth's cruel fate

I'm a sweetless piñata made from yesterday's news
a faithless vow
empty as a church

she's all deceit
a deep, salted wound
a prick and prod production
of hell's delight

FREE WILL IS A BITCH

labor under misconceptions
pretty lies you've built of dust
creosote of good intentions
ashes of a naïve trust

grovel to unholy masters
little gods and little men
architects of bright disasters
peddlers of a violent zen

murder lovers with presumptions
bleed from them each ounce of joy
revel in each cool consumption
savor all you would destroy

bury mercy in your madness
lock away your foolish dream
coat each word in sugared sadness
swallow every empty scream

gamble on your fallen brothers
tiny men with tiny minds
ransom off the sin of others
freedom is the tie that binds

WOUNDED, WORTHLESS
& WEARY

wounded, I have bent to taste
the crimson liquid of Your grace
Your wind-worn flesh, the thorny brow
which marked Your kingship then and now

worthless, I have taken hold
the threads of mercy from Your robe
Your ruined hands, Your gaping side
and pledged myself Your sullied bride

weary, I have given up
the poison of my rightful cup
the curse of death, the shroud of sin
to die and, in You, live again

photo by Holly Thrasher

J. Patrick Lemarr is a poet and the author of "Fallen" (2005) and "I Am A Broken House" (2011). A minister and former educator, Lemarr resides in Grand Prairie, Texas with his wife and three children.

www.jpatricklemarr.com
www.twitter.com/jpatricklemarr

Worlds Apart

a fantasy novel from **J. Patrick Lemarr**

Coming 2012